STEAMPUNK
BIRDS COLORING BOOK

✓ **45** adorable **coloring** pages
✓ **Great for aspiring** adults **and teens**
✓ **Ideal for** colored **pencils, markers or pencils**
✓ Large **print page** format: **8.5 x 11 inches**
✓ **Single-sided** pages **to avoid spills, ensuring your** masterpieces stay clean

We appreciate you selecting our book, buying our coloring book, and helping our tiny business.

We wish you joy when coloring! We thank all of the contributors to this book for their generosity.

On our Amazon website, kindly post a review and some of your lovely colored photos.